THE AUTHOR AND HIS AUDIENCE

the author and his audience

63674

With a chronology
of major events in the publishing history of
J. B. Lippincott Company

PUBLISHED BY J. B. LIPPINCOTT COMPANY ON
THE OCCASION OF ITS 175TH ANNIVERSARY

contents

foreword
the author and his audience
medical publishing
educational publishing
chronology

foreword

IT MAY COME as a surprise to some, not that we are publishing a special book to commemorate the 175th Anniversary of J. B. Lippincott Company, but that we are publishing a book that is not a history. Certainly there is a long, rich and exciting story to tell in the development of this firm from a Philadelphia bookstore which issued an occasional book on its own when George Washington was President of the United States, to a major publisher in the medical, nursing and educational fields, and in general trade adult and children's books.

In 1867, when Joshua Ballinger Lippincott was asked by a friend whom he was escorting through the offices and plant of his seventy-five-year-old firm why he did not write its history, he pointed across a city-block-sized room filled with desks to the only partitioned section in the whole building—the private office of the publisher and owner—and remarked: "Could I relate the scenes that have occurred in that room you would fully appreciate the annoyances and trials of a publisher's life. But its mysteries are sacred; and the blank, sad histories of would-be authors and the little foibles of the really great authors must all slumber there untold."

In 1899, more than a decade after Joshua Lippincott's death, a disastrous fire completely destroyed the Lippincott publishing offices, warehouse and plant. Records of over a century were lost, and these untold tales of literary achievements, aspirations and disappointments were buried in the rubble and debris.

Although some of the scenes that occurred in Joshua Lippincott's private office may have been lost forever when the walls fell in, much has been reconstructed and when added to the history of the firm's next sixty-eight years makes a substantial contribution to any story of publishing in the United States. It was decided, however, that while publishing-company histories are of interest to the publishing world, to historians, and to some authors, they do not have broad appeal to those whose interest in books is more personal than technical, more subjective than professional. We concluded that perhaps an informal essay on the publishing process by which the author reaches his reader would be not only interesting to a large number of book-oriented people but useful as well to students and others who want a bird's-eye view of the writing-publishing-marketing scene.

In *The Author and His Audience* the "Author" is the writer of general trade books, both adult and juvenile, and the "Audience" is the entire English-speaking world. Since J. B. Lippincott Company's publications cover such numerous and vast specialized areas, it would seem opportune to include equal emphasis on medical or nursing or educational publishing. However, to reach the interest of the largest number, it was decided to focus on the publishing of general literature, the field in which books are reviewed and advertised in the general press, are shown in bookstore windows, and dominate the shelves of public and school libraries.

Yet, because they are so vital a part of the Lippincott business and because a number of their titles are marketed through so-called trade channels, it seemed of interest to include brief résumés of Lippincott's educational and medical divisions as the operation of each pertains to the subject of this anniversary essay.

—J.W.L., Jr.

the author and his audience

Introduction

WHAT FOLLOWS is an attempt to trace the line of communication running from the writer to the reader—specifically, from the writer of books to his audience. Most prominent in this line of communication is the publisher, who makes the editorial decisions, pays the costs of publication and the authors' royalties, and tries through all available channels to bring each of his books to the attention of the widest possible audience and to induce in that audience the desire to read the books on his list. There are many important influences along the line: advance readers, booksellers, book reviewers and editors of periodicals that contain book reviews, teachers, public and school librarians, book clubs, and, most important of all, the audience itself, which grows or languishes according to the degree of its own contagious enthusiasm.

A publishing house could not exist without authors, and the first thing to do is to express appreciation of the relationship we at J. B. Lippincott Company enjoy with the authors on our list—a relationship that includes a vivid sense of obligation, of mutual confidence and understanding, a common experience of shared triumphs and disappointments—in a word, partnership. To list all our authors would be equivalent to reprinting our general catalogue, and it is with no lack of appreciation of those who are not named here that we mention especially some who have been with us longest and have contributed most to the continuity of the Company since we celebrated our sesquicentennial in 1942.

We have published ten of Hal Borland's books, including two reissued from other publishers' lists, and all of them are in print. Of Richard Lockridge, including both his own books and those written in collaboration with the late Frances Lockridge, we have published about five million words and have enjoyed every one of them. Mary O'Hara and Betty MacDonald are to come in for later attention—so are the Pulitzer Prize winners Harper Lee and Leon Edel. Betty MacDonald's sister Mary Bard has had successful books both for adults and for children, and Molly Costain Haycraft has ably cultivated both fields. So have James Ramsey Ullman, whose *Age of Mountaineering* is a classic, and Louise Dickinson Rich, who took to the woods in Maine. Elizabeth Gray Vining has written memorably of Japanese royalty and American Quakers, of John Donne and Flora MacDonald. Gladys Denny Shultz's first book, *Letters to Jane,* was published in 1948, revised in 1960, and is still in print—as are several others by this versatile writer. Another versatile writer is Gladys Taber, best known for her Stillmeadow books, with the distinction of having a novel in print for ten years. Three books by Marya Mannes bring us the candid comments of a distinguished observer; three by Charles W. Morton present the life and opinions of the most Bostonian editor ever to have come from Nebraska. The recent arrival from another publisher's orbit of Hildegarde Dolson, with her delightful novel *Open the Door,* was an unexpected pleasure. And a single abandoned egg hatched *That Quail, Robert* along with 90,000 copies of Margaret Stanger's book.

John Keats, John Bakeless, and John J. Pullen combine distinction with popularity, covering among them a wide spectrum of American life and history. Similarly, in fiction, Shirley Seifert's dozen novels reanimate the American past, while Lane Kauffmann's half dozen illuminate the present. Stanley Loomis is following up *Du Barry* and *Paris in the Terror* with another exploration of French history—this time an episode from the nineteenth century. Geddes MacGregor has written brilliantly on both secular and religious subjects. And we are particularly happy to have published *The Beloved Invader,* the first novel by the distinguished writer of religious books, Eugenia Price.

From England we have John Moore, as delightful for *You English Words* as for his best-selling novel, *The Waters under the Earth;* P. H. Newby, called by *The New Yorker* "the most interesting and intellectually distinguished English writer to have come into view since the end of the Second World War"; and Doris Langley Moore, expert on Byron and Marie Bashkirtseff; and for superlative entertainment, Celia Fremlin, with six novels of suspense, all uniquely original, from *The Hours before Dawn* to *Prisoner's Base.* Dudley Pope is the author of five naval histories, which have established his distinguished reputation in this field: his latest book is a novel, *Ramage,* a story of naval action during the Napoleonic Wars.

And looking to the future, we expect more distinguished novels from four writers who skipped the "promising" period and produced solid achievements with their first novels: Myron Kaufmann, Carter Wilson, Nicholas Delbanco, and—with a second fine book already to his credit—Thomas Pynchon.

These acknowledgments could be continued indefinitely, but our authors who write for children have been waiting long enough for recognition. Books for children have greater longevity than those written for their elders, so that successful authors of children's books pile up tens and dozens of books that stay in print indefinitely, attracting generation after generation. There are some versatile geniuses, like Phyllis McGinley and John Ciardi, who write expertly in prose and in verse. There is Hugh Lofting, whose Doctor Dolittle is among the immortals. There are Munro Leaf and Lois Lenski, who in different ways introduce children to the realities they are going to face. Mabel Leigh Hunt has written for children at several age levels and has sixteen books in print. Books that tell boys and girls what animals are really like have come in welcome abundance from Joseph W. Lippincott and Harold McCracken. Mystery stories for young readers arrive regularly from Elizabeth Honness, Irene Bowen, and Mary C. Jane; similarly, stories of sports from Curtis Bishop and Burgess Leonard.

Writers who make knowledge exciting include Richard Headstrom, Duane Bradley, Arthur H. Klein, Edwin Hoag, and Raymond A. Wohlrabe. (The last named, and many other distinguished authors, have contributed to the Portraits of the Nations Series.) Elizabeth Ripley introduces young readers to the great names in painting and sculpture. Joseph Leeming has a dozen book on how to have fun with household objects.

There are many authors whose books are living after them and who should be saluted here. Hugh Lofting has been mentioned. Betty MacDonald and Miriam Clark Potter created memorable characters in Mrs. Piggle-Wiggle and Mrs. Goose. Rosamond du Jardin delighted many thousands of readers with her understanding stories of girls growing in and out of their teens. Several generations of young readers have enjoyed Helen Fuller Orton's mysteries. John J. Floherty was one of our oldest friends and most valued authors—he wrote of everything from skin diving to jet propulsion. Seventeen of his books are in print. Eleanor Farjeon's poems and her Martin Pippin stories will live indefinitely.

And now the authors who have most recently joined us and who have attracted audiences eager for their future work. Jeannette Eyerly has taken up where Rosamond du Jardin left off in teen-age fiction, with perceptive novels on the problems faced by today's youth. Susan Purdy combines colorful illustrations with clever and amusing ideas, and Theodora Koob brings the Revolutionary period alive in her historical narratives. Kaye

Starbird's books of verse delight a widening audience. The stories of our English authors, Nina Bawden, Veronica Robinson, and Philippa Pearce, are rich in characterization and suspense. And to think that we haven't mentioned *The Secret Garden* or *Little Black Sambo*.

I

IN 1965 more than twenty thousand new books were published in the United States, plus another eighty-five hundred new editions. Who reads all these books? And, for that matter, who writes them?

As to the first question, taken statistically, there is no difficulty. There are plenty of people. No logical reason why a population of almost two hundred million should not manage to absorb the output—there are almost ten thousand people to each new title. But logic does not correspond to reality: there are numerous reasons why in fact the population does not absorb the output. Although a vast amount of reading, especially in schools and colleges, is compulsory, there are many millions among our two hundred million who never read books at all. Americans read fewer books per capita than Englishmen, Frenchmen, Germans, Norwegians, Swedes, Danes, and several other national populations. In some cases, many fewer. This is the only aspect in which the relation of the number of books published to the size of the population has any significance. Americans read less than other educated people.

Whatever the size of our population, altogether apart from statistics, common sense makes it clear beyond dispute that too many books are published. If this were not true, then not so many new books would subside so rapidly into oblivion. Some books are stillborn, and very few of them are neglected master-pieces. (Occasionally a masterpiece is neglected at publication and discovered later. *Moby Dick* is an example. But it was by no means received in silence when it was issued in 1851.) To offset the depressing spectacle—if something so nearly invisible can be called a spectacle—of the stillborn books, there are always some which achieve immortality. The two questions posed at the outset might be said to encompass the life of a book from birth to death, making honorable exception for the books which do not die. Actually, the point of raising them was to introduce a discussion of the relationship between writers and readers.

One great difference, obvious but not often remarked upon, lies in the relationship of time. You can read a novel of average length in a few hours—four or five hours at the relatively un-demanding rate of a page a minute. How long did it take the author to write it? Certainly several hundred hours—possibly even a thousand or more. Of course there are some, like the late Edgar Wallace, who can turn out a book a month: the output of Erle Stanley Gardner, including his pseudonymous alter ego, A. A. Fair, is less than that but still stupendous. And even at the rate of a book every thousand hours, an experienced, profes-sional writer can make the time count. A five-day week, four hours a day, with two weeks off for vacation, makes up the thousand hours in a year. And at only a page an hour, the production comes to a thousand pages a year. This is not merely to play with numbers. One of the most prolific novelists who ever lived, Sir Walter Scott, turned out long novels at frequent intervals while carrying on several other activities. However, such fertility as his and Trollope's is normally possible only to diarists.

The writer's working hours are lonely hours. Some people can concentrate in the midst of chaos and bedlam, but not many of them are writers. A writer has to work where he is not subject to interruption or disturbance. Since he is working in solitude, he is peculiarly subject to misgivings: "Is what I am writing any good?" Moreover, the optimistic production estimates in the preceding paragraph took little account of the time needed for revision, for reconsideration, for discarding, for rewriting. Still less for letting the cistern refill between books—or, if need be, between chapters. Among distinguished American novelists who have pursued their profession with regularity, the late J. P. Marquand turned out a novel every couple of years; Louis Auchincloss seems to do about the same; James Gould Cozzens publishes much less frequently. Ernest Hemingway wrote only six novels altogether (in addition to his short stories and his nonfiction, and including *The Old Man and the Sea* but not *The Torrents of Spring*). Faulkner published at irregular intervals, sometimes yearly, sometimes longer.

Perhaps it is frivolous, though there seems to be an element of justice in it, to speculate on the novelist's rewards in terms of hours spent by his readers in proportion to those spent by himself. Ten thousand readers at five hours each is fifty times the thousand hours the author is assumed to have put in. A hundred thousand readers gives a ratio of five hundred to one. For writers like Conrad and Henry James, the number of hours spent by readers is constantly enlarged with the addition of new generations, and perhaps raised to a power by the biographers and critics who have written books about them.

So far this discussion has been confined to novelists. In general it may apply to journalistic nonfiction. But nonfiction writing which requires research is in a different class altogether. Not only in consideration of the time spent in the search directly related to the book, but in all the specialized training which gave the author the ability to tackle his subject in the first place.

Now then, back to the statistics for a moment. Of the 20,000 new books (excluding new editions) published in 1965, 1,615 were novels or books of short stories, at least 6,000 more were in categories of nonfiction of interest to the general public, and 2,473 were books for children. Most of the rest were technical or otherwise specialized publications. So were some of the general nonfiction titles, depending on subject and nature of treatment. We can only guess at the number of nonfiction titles of limited or specialized interest, since the published statistics do not distinguish books issued by commercial publishers from those issued by university presses in such categories as history, biography, and literature. Say 4,000 of the 6,000 nonfiction titles were published for the general reader at the adult level. In relation to what was actually written, the published titles represent the visible part of the iceberg. Nobody knows how many manuscripts go unpublished, but any publisher who has to deal with unsolicited manuscripts will agree that the iceberg comparison is reasonable. So when we asked, "Who writes all these books?" we ignored a vast unknown quantity of books that never see print.

II

UNPUBLISHABLE MANUSCRIPTS range from the hopelessly inept to the borderline cases. The latter are books which have merit, but not enough. Commercial publishers will consider them both for their literary quality and their chance of making a profit or at least breaking even. Every publisher will take a manuscript which shows dubious signs of commercial success provided that its quality is sufficiently distinguished, especially if the publisher believes that the author will produce more books and make a name for himself. The borderline case that fails to find a publisher will probably have gone through a year of submissions before the author or his agent is discouraged enough to withdraw it; and the author is lucky if the time required to come to a decision on each submission is only three to four weeks. For one thing, it is the borderline case that calls for the largest number of readings by the publisher's editorial staff before the decision is made. For another, all publishers' machinery is constantly clogged up by the endless flow of unsolicited ineptitudes.

And these are the vast majority. Who writes them? Almost everybody, if you go by categories—housewives, professional men, prisoners, the unemployed, the employed, whatever you can think of—but fortunately not everybody in every category. It may not be long until a publisher's receptionist is startled by the appearance of a passenger from a flying saucer, holding a manuscript and saying, "Take me to your reader." Perhaps the reason why the U.S.A. lags behind other nations in book-reading is that so many people are trying to write and have no time left over for reading. One wishes that occasionally an unsuccessful writer might be struck by the idea, based on his own experience, that the time he spends writing diminishes the success of the writers who are published. More likely, when the unsuccessful writer does read a current book, he is frustrated and infuriated by the conviction that it is not as good as his own stuff.

Unsolicited material is in general unpromising. Where, then, do publishers find the books they publish? First, a definition of "unsolicited." The term does not apply to manuscripts submitted by accredited literary agents. The fact that such an agent is submitting a manuscript means that it has been through the agent's screening process. Moreover, publishers solicit manuscripts from agents. Agents have their own opinions of publishers, specifically of the kinds of books each publisher handles most successfully, and an intelligent publisher does not ask an agent to submit material that is clearly outside his range of interest. Still, there are many well-known instances where a book, later successful, is declined by several publishers. Such was the case with *Under the Volcano,* by Malcolm Lowry. Perhaps this is too unusual to be a very good example, but it is too interesting to omit. The author's agent submitted it to twelve publishers in 1941, and after all of them had declined it, he returned it to the author. Four years later it was back in the agent's hands, considerably rewritten, and was placed with Reynal & Hitchcock, who published it in 1947. Its reputation grew over the years, and eventually, after being out of print, it was reissued in 1965 by one of the publishers that had turned it down twenty-four years earlier: J. B. Lippincott Company.

Lippincott has taken books turned down by others and rejoiced to see them become outstanding best sellers (*Earth and High Heaven,* by Gwethalyn Graham, for one, among others) and has turned down books that have skyrocketed elsewhere. In the latter category there have been novels of a sensational, soap-opera character, which needed sensational exploitation; in these cases we do not regret our decisions. There have also been a few books we lost because we underestimated their distinction. These we do regret.

A book which we had the gumption to accept, without knowing we were not the first to have been approached, was the all-time number-one Lippincott best seller, *The Egg and I,* by Betty MacDonald, published in October, 1945, and destined for a sale in the U.S.A. and Canada of over 1,801,450 copies, including book club and paperback, but not including over 300,000 copies of a condensation. The regular Lippincott hardbound edition had sold 760,501 copies as of August, 1966. Consideration of *The Egg and I* leads in two directions—and we cannot follow one to the end of the line without retracing our steps and making progress along the other.

Let's start with the direction which led to the acceptance of the book. A new point is to be made here: although *The Egg and I* was the work of a new author, previously unpublished, it was submitted in unfinished form. It came to us in the form of a detailed synoptic outline. Now this form of submission has always been customary for new books by published authors. In the twenty-one years since *The Egg and I* was published, it has become increasingly prevalent for new authors as well. This is in line with the increasing competition among publishers for new books and new authors, a subject for later discussion. For now, let us say that the procedure makes sense for nonfiction, where an outline can with substantial accuracy cover the subject in advance, and where a couple of completed chapters can give an adequate idea of the style of the complete book. In fiction, samples may not so trustworthily represent what is to come. Indeed, the better the novel, the more likely it is to take off on its own, to take off with the author's imagination like a runaway horse, to live its own life. Novels are often contracted for, nowadays, on the basis of an outline and a few sample chapters: lucky the publisher whose author *does* kick over the traces. (Usually.)

The other direction has to do with the consequences. After *The Egg and I* was published, manuscripts in imitation of it were submitted to us in suffocating quantities. The more imitative, the less likely they were to make the grade. But there were a few which fell into the same category without being imitative —we began calling them "funny women" books. Betty Mac-Donald herself wrote three more, and they were by far the best. Of the other funny women, we were successful with several. One in particular may be recalled without being named. Her first book was under consideration when Mr. J. W. Lippincott,

Sr., on being casually notified and informally consulted, remarked, "Well, you never make money off the books you turn down." So we took it and it sold over 30,000 copies. (There is an obvious corollary to Mr. Lippincott's remark, and if he had felt the other way he would have turned it the other way.)

III

NOT ONLY is it true that many books are offered to publishers before they are finished—some of them in the initial stage of composition, others when not a word is on paper. With increasing competition among themselves, publishers must put up with this—they have, if not individually, collectively asked for it. Moreover, publishers are themselves continually originating ideas for books and finding authors who are willing to take the assignments if the advance against royalties is sufficient.

Another source consists of tips from the editor's friends, including his authors. The editor wants to be the first to get the tip, because otherwise it may be too late; therefore he must always be prepared to make decisions on partial material plus his own imagination. Often authors of textbooks know of colleagues who are writing—textbooks perhaps, or maybe trade books, that is, books for the general reading public. Authors know other authors—one is likely to know when another is dissatisfied with his publisher and ready for a change. This may lead to discreet seduction. However, publishers with ideas for books most frequently approach writers who are independent of publishing ties, and authors who accommodate their publishers by acting as talent scouts usually work in uncultivated fields.

Editors in publishing houses get ideas for books, or for authors, or for both at once, from reading newspapers, magazines, newsletters, third-class mail, ticker tape, or whatever else. Most editors gravitate into their jobs because they are compulsive readers. They would rather read the label on a bottle of Angostura Bitters than look at a sunset. The man who prefers the sunset is the author. If he looks at sunrises, he is a nature writer, and his publisher is lucky to have him.

Most of all, the source of books for a publisher's list is the output of his own established authors. This begs the question— how does an author become established in the first place? There are various ways: writing for newspapers, writing for magazines; teaching conspicuously or attracting attention in public service (it being assumed that anyone in these categories is literate); almost any way except one. That is to write a book-length manuscript which goes the rounds with no takers.

Often it happens that a borderline manuscript will lead an editor to propose that if the author will follow certain suggestions for revision, the manuscript will be reconsidered. The proposal may go so far as to include an offer of a modest advance against future royalties, to be kept by the author whether the revised manuscript is accepted or not. Above the borderline is the manuscript which the editor does not wish to risk losing, although he knows it needs further work: he contracts for the book and relies on his powers of persuasion and diplomacy to get the work done. Below the borderline is the manuscript in which no editor has sufficient confidence to justify working with the author.

Without such confidence, an editor is in no position to make suggestions. Moreover, he hesitates to criticize a rejected manuscript on another ground: the advice he gives might run contrary to the ideas of the next editor to whom the manuscript is submitted, an editor who could conceivably be interested in developing it. These, plus pressure of time, are the reasons why publishers cannot criticize unsolicited manuscripts, although they are constantly besought for advice by disappointed authors.

IV

THIS SITUATION leads to a demand for editorial advice and assistance on another basis. Over the last few decades editorial services for amateur writers who wish to become professional writers have multiplied rapidly. These services take two principal forms: the writers' conference, generally held in the summer for a few weeks in attractive natural settings and usually in connection with a college or university; and the creative writing course, which is part of an academic curriculum. Possibly the schools of journalism, originally graduate schools of universities, provided the model for courses and seminars in creative writing. These are conducted by one or more members of the regular faculty; in addition, there has developed a new idea, the "writer in residence," an established writer who lives on the campus for a semester or a year and is available for literary discussion of every variety. As to the writers' conferences, the prototype was established over forty years ago at Bread Loaf, in Vermont. The Bread Loaf Writers' Conference was created more or less accidentally, when Middlebury College inherited a hotel and cottages on Bread Loaf Mountain and had to find a use for them. The admirable Bread Loaf School of English of Middlebury College became a feature of the summer season and has remained so—but this left a couple of weeks over at the end of August. A small staff of authors and publishers was assembled, and writers were invited to bring their manuscripts for reading and criticism, also to enjoy the benefits of instruction and entertainment provided by the lectures of the staff. Some of these have been known to wheel freely. Also, Bread Loaf was fortunate in having Robert Frost as a writer in residence, since he lived only a few miles away and used to come over frequently, if not daily. (It is said that the Conference was started at his suggestion.) Bread Loaf also attracted unknown writers by establishing a system of fellowships. Each year a few writers who have made a start, or at least shown promise, are selected on the recommendation of professional editors and invited to participate in the activities of the conference as guests. Directors have included the publisher John Farrar, Theodore Morrison of the Harvard faculty, and the present incumbent, John Ciardi, who has nine books on the Lippincott list.

The Bread Loaf Writers' Conference has served as the model for many others all over the country. The *Saturday Review* annually publishes a list of them, with their dates and programs. In 1966 there were thirty listed, each lasting one to three weeks, plus fourteen of briefer duration. The value of writers' conferences and of courses in creative writing has been debated, and the debate will continue as long as there is something to be said on both sides. Some writers have assuredly been helped; others have not. Among the latter, many are obviously beyond helping; but as long as they are determined to write and have no other means of getting their writing criticized, even if the criticism is discouraging, there will be a place for creative writing courses and writers' conferences. In any event, nothing whatever will stop them.

Can writing be taught? Certainly not to the untalented. Perhaps, strictly speaking, writing cannot be *taught* to anybody. Much can be learned, however, by talented but inexperienced writers—from other writers, from critics who give courses in creative writing or who are on the staffs of writers' conferences. Perhaps most of all can be learned in solitude, just by reading.

On the positive side, many instances of success could be

given. A conspicuous example was Mary O'Hara's first novel, *My Friend Flicka,* which has sold 360,000 in the publisher's edition, plus 50,000 in the Armed Forces edition and 600,000 in book club editions—over a million altogether—since its publication in 1941. It was first a short story written at Mary O'Hara's ranch in Wyoming. Two years later, in New York, she attended a class given by Whit Burnett, editor of *Story* magazine and of Story Press, which was also at that time a source of books for J. B. Lippincott Company. He read the story and brought it to Lippincott, whose editors asked the author to expand it into a novel. At her hesitancy in undertaking anything so difficult, the editors promised help, but she refused to sign a contract until she had tried herself out thoroughly. She vanished into the deep New England countryside, eventually returning with sufficient material for three books—and the courage to undertake the project. Whit Burnett was her special editor and stood by with advice, encouragement, and criticism while she produced three novels, *My Friend Flicka, Thunderhead,* and *Green Grass of Wyoming.*

This and some other examples which might be supplied suggest that there is an advantage to the author when the course in creative writing is given by a professional editor. In any event, many courses are given by professional writers of high standing; and any recognized course or conference is regularly courted by editors, who are likely to give earliest consideration to manuscripts coming with a recommendation from these sources.

In fact, courses and conferences have become so well established that one wonders how earlier generations got along without them. Dickens never went to a writers' conference, and Jane Austen never took a course in creative writing. Nor did Hemingway or Willa Cather or Sinclair Lewis.

V

NOW, as we approach our own generation, we reach the editor, who in the last forty years has assumed an increasingly active role. The best-known example is the late Maxwell Perkins of Scribners, whose contribution to his authors' success in handling their material has been widely recognized; the record is available in his letters, *Editor to Author,* where his intimate editorial relationship is recorded with writers from Scott Fitzgerald to James Jones, and especially with Thomas Wolfe. Wolfe himself wrote in detail of what Perkins did for *Look Homeward, Angel* in *The Story of a Novel.*

It is instructive to compare the Wolfe-Perkins relationship with another celebrated author-editor relationship only thirty years earlier: that of Joseph Conrad and Edward Garnett. First of all, Conrad, far from any opportunity to get literary advice or criticism of any kind—he even had had to teach himself English —wrote his first novel, *Almayer's Folly,* over a period of several years. He has told in *A Personal Record* how he carried the unfinished manuscript of *Almayer* on various voyages, including the trip up the Congo that resulted in *Heart of Darkness,* and how he finally showed it to a passenger with whom he had previously been unacquainted, and who laconically but emphatically advised Conrad to finish it. Conrad in many ways had a life of discomfort and disappointment, but in one respect his good fortune was miraculous: his first novel, upon its submission to Dent, was read by Edward Garnett, who became Conrad's editor and intimate friend. The story of their relationship is in the volume of Conrad's letters to Garnett, with Garnett's long introduction. The entire story is fascinating, but the point here is that Garnett read, encouraged, recommended publication—but apparently suggested no changes, although the narrative is frequently obscure. (He even let Conrad use "like" as a conjunction, and in the next novel, *An Outcast of the Islands,* there appears the phrase "except he.") In those days an author was supposed to write his own book, and publishers could take it or leave it. Garnett was not even an editor in the present sense of the word. He was a "publisher's reader," leading a semi-detached existence and working at home, but he became the intimate and indispensable friend of many distinguished writers besides Conrad.

The Perkins-Wolfe relationship was an extreme case of an author's dependence on an editor, and as different from Conrad's relationship to Garnett as anything could be. The story is too well known to need more than a synopsis here: Wolfe had started as a playwright, had studied at Harvard with George Pierce Baker in the famous 47 Workshop—a practical course in dramatic technique that was another forerunner of creative writing courses. He turned to fiction in the late twenties (his as well as the century's) and produced a mass of autobiographical material which was declined by several publishers before Perkins saw its possibilities. What Perkins did is recorded in the books mentioned earlier—as James Thurber's ballplayer said, you could look it up.

Between these extremes, the editorial process may take any form. It may be a salvage operation—an attempt to make a publishable book out of a manuscript which demonstrates the author's inability to bring off what he signed up to do. This process may well involve the services of an anonymous free lance who knows how to rewrite. This entails an unforeseen expense which must be negotiated between the publisher and the (ostensible) author. The case may be so hopeless that the publisher abandons the manuscript as unsatisfactory (most publishers' contracts with authors allow for this contingency) and, depending on the terms of the original agreement, forfeits any
advances already paid.

More often, and happily for all, the editor works as much for the author's benefit as for the publisher's, if not more. A professional author needs only to have the kind of questions raised that will recall his attention to what he may have written inattentively or inadvertently. The editor's eye should be focused upon the author's intention. Is the author's meaning clear? Are there details resulting from carelessness or fatigue—repetitions, contradictions, clichés—which may easily be adjusted? Here again, Maxwell Perkins's letters—to other authors as well as Thomas Wolfe: Marcia Davenport, for instance—demonstrate supremely well what needs doing and what can be done. Put it that the function of the editor on this level is to forestall as far as possible the *avoidable* faults that would be criticized by reviewers of the book. But in all specific instances on this level, the decision must be the author's.

There have been notable instances of editor-author relationships where mutual confidence has been both an effect and a cause of intelligent cooperation, where the editor's understanding of the author's intentions and his ability to keep his own ego out of the situation combine to help the author to realize his intentions most successfully. The late Saxe Commins worked with William Faulkner through many books; a similar close relationship existed between Pascal Covici and John Steinbeck.

Now for the story of a first novel where the genius of the author was unmistakable from the outset, and where the editor was able to provide, by criticism and suggestion, what would otherwise have been available only through the trial and error of protracted experience. In 1960 J. B. Lippincott Company published Harper Lee's first novel, *To Kill a Mockingbird*. This was the outcome of a set of circumstances that had begun a year or two previously, when an early version of the manuscript was submitted to Lippincott by the author's agent, under the title "Atticus." The Lippincott editors recognized something beyond talent—genius is not an extravagant word—in the material; but the better the material, the more important that the technique and the organization should do it justice. A Lippincott editor who had worked with many successful authors, including Gwethalyn Graham and Pat Frank, worked closely with Harper Lee on the revision. Here is the editor's reply to an inquiring correspondent, reprinted with Miss Lee's permission.

Before answering your letter, I wanted to make sure Harper Lee would not object to my describing to you something about her experiences in the final writing of *To Kill a Mockingbird*. She herself would do a much better job of what it was like.

First of all, the element in the original manuscript which was unmistakable: it was alive, the characters stood on their own two feet, they were three-dimensional. And the spark of the true writer flashed in every line.

Though Miss Lee had then never published even an essay or a short story, this was clearly not the work of an amateur or tyro. And indeed, she had written constantly since her very early childhood. It was difficult at first to understand why she had resisted the temptation to try, at least, for publication, but as I grew to know her better, I came to believe the cause lay in an innate humility and a deep respect for the art of writing. To put it another way, what she wanted with all her being was to *write*—not merely to "be a writer." She had learned the essential part of her craft, with no so-called professional help, simply by working at it and working at it, endlessly.

However, the manuscript we saw was more a series of anecdotes than a fully conceived novel. The editorial call to duty was plain. She needed, at last, professional help in organizing her material and developing a sound plot structure.

After a couple of false starts, the story-line, interplay of characters, and fall of emphasis grew clearer, and with each revision—there were many minor changes as the story grew in strength and in her own vision of it—the true stature of the novel became evident.

We saw a great deal of each other during this period, and, if conditions make it possible, I believe such close, frequent communication can be of enormous benefit to the author, the book, and incidentally to the editor. But of course writing is the loneliest of activities. Harper Lee literally spent her days and nights in the most intense efforts to set down what she wanted to say in the way which would best say it to a reader. You ask for "chapter and verse." That's a bit hard. It's no secret that she was living on next to nothing and in considerable physical discomfort while she was writing *Mockingbird*. I don't think anyone, certainly not I, ever heard one small mutter of discontent throughout all those months of writing and tearing up, writing and tearing up.

And you ask how she responded to my criticisms. Well, with intelligence, naturally, but one expects that, never mind how often one may be disappointed. When she disagreed with a suggestion, we talked it out, sometimes for hours. And sometimes she came around to my way of thinking, sometimes I to hers, sometimes the discussion would open up an entirely new line of country. I think I can say with truth that she always knew I was in her corner, even when I was most critical, which is really all there is to say about the editor's part in the success of *Mockingbird*. As you know, the sole function of an editor is to help a writer bring forth the best book in him. Unless a writer will totally commit himself to the same end, the editor must be content with mid-wifing a disappointingly puny child. It is because, and only because, Harper Lee did so totally commit herself that *Mockingbird* reveals a remarkable talent at its (then) best. If sales had stopped at 3000, that statement would still stand. Since I believe that her total commitment to her writing is an enduring quality, I have no fear for her future.

VI

TO RESUME: a book is accepted, the manuscript is brought to completion and edited, publication is scheduled for six or eight or ten months later (depending on whether the material is to be serialized before it appears as a book; whether there are delays in manufacturing, because of illustrations or indexing or other difficulties; or depending on favorable marketing conditions in relation to season). Then what? Then there are technicalities. First, the manuscript must be copy-edited. This is an altogether different process from editing, and while it has another purpose and requires a set of abilities altogether different from the editor's, nevertheless the copy-editor, patient, objective, uninvolved, and often at least faintly contemptuous, discovers things in the manuscript which need attention and which the editor is embarrassed to have overlooked. Copy-editing has been distinguished from editing in an essay which, while hardly of classic distinction, serves our purpose as well as anything we can readily find. It was published by Rutgers University Press in a symposium called *Bookmaking and Kindred Amenities* and is quoted here by kind permission, with slight adaptations.

Copy-editing "requires a careful and methodical mind, capable of sustained attention which must frequently be applied to the dullest sorts of reading matter, and a memory which can recall, when the editor spots the word *maneuver* on page 112 of a manuscript, that the author spelled it *manoeuvre* on page 63, or that *nuance* was italicized on page 46 when *coup d'état* turns up in roman and with no accent on 245. . . .

"It takes an editor whose own name ends in *s* to handle the problems raised by plurals and possessives. Such a simple matter as *Keeping up with the Joneses* usually emerges as *Keeping up with the Jones', Keeping up with the Jones's,* or *Keeping up with the Jone's,* and *Jones's wife* is more commonly *Jones' wife* or *Jone's wife;* it is a cagey author who calls her Mrs. Jones and avoids all the pitfalls."

An experienced copy-editor has commented professionally on the foregoing as follows:

"The examples given are effective in showing the kind of attention required of a copy-editor, but the problems they represent are not statistically the most prevalent. I believe most copy-editors would agree that from the standpoint of frequency of occurrence and difficulty of solution the three areas of greatest concern are numbers (whether words or figures), capitalization, and compounds (*proof reader, proof-reader, proofreader*). Another thing copy-editors do that deserves mention is to keep track of personal and place names in fiction. Authors are forgetful enough to make this almost a necessity."

The next mechanical process is production—specifically, the conversion of a single typescript, edited, revised, copy-edited, with front matter (title page, contents, dedication, etc.), with or without illustrations, bibliography, notes, index, appendices, whatever else, into several thousand printed and bound volumes. But this is a mechanical process in literal terms only. First of all it requires a castoff, or estimate of the number of characters, i.e., letters, punctuation marks, and spaces in the manuscript. Then the design, which is anything but mechanical. The designer must choose the face and size of type in relation to the number of characters in the manuscript and the number of pages desired in the finished book. Several considerations enter in, principally legibility and cost. The designer lays out the title page, the rest of the special matter, the binding stamps (or dies), all in relation so that the book is an aesthetic unit and not a hodgepodge of disjunctive elements like a beatnik's wardrobe.

Then the quantity to be ordered for the first printing must be settled, and the production costs estimated, in relation to expected sales and the maximum retail price considered acceptable by those members of the publisher's staff who will be responsible for selling the book. These decisions made and jobs accomplished, the manuscript is ready to be set in type. Now suppliers must be lined up for typesetting, plates, paper, printing, binding—all within schedule and budget. Few publishers do their own manufacturing: most publishers who designate themselves as The Something Press are perhaps, though no doubt unconsciously, inaccurate. University presses, however, are usually entitled to the designation, since most universities maintain printing plants if only to produce catalogues and examination papers.

While the book is being manufactured, a process goes on that began when the accepted manuscript was completed (or vice versa): the attempt to find a market for the book, meaning people who will read this particular book—people who will even buy it.

Who are these people? Parts of the answer are obvious: educational textbooks are read by students in schools and colleges; medical books by doctors, nurses, medical students; children's books by children, also by their parents and teachers and by librarians who read aloud to children. For the trade book addressed to the general adult reader, the audience is unpredictable. This makes the lives of trade publishers simultaneously frustrating and fascinating.

VII

OF COURSE a new book by an established author will be read by that author's following. But how did the author become established? Every author is unknown to begin with—unless he was known in some other capacity.

So let us begin with a hypothetical book by a writer previously unknown to the reading public. If the book is nonfiction, dealing with a subject which has required the author to dig for his facts, then the author presumably has a professional or quasi-professional standing—as a newspaperman or a teacher, for instance; and if so, he is known at least to the circle of his colleagues. It may well have been one of his colleagues who brought his manuscript to the publisher's attention in the first place. Even a first novelist may have influential friends, and certainly has if he came to the publisher under the auspices of one of the creative-writing courses or one of the writers' conferences which publishers take seriously. But he is still unknown to the people who are going—or who the author and publisher hope are going—to read his book.

The book begins, then, with the impetus of the publisher's enthusiasm. This enthusiasm may arise from either artistic or commercial considerations. A manuscript may appeal to the publisher though its commercial prospects are doubtful because it is in his opinion the work of a highly promising talent, which may be expected to develop and, who knows, even eventually to develop profitably; or it may be a promising piece of merchandise with no literary distinction or chance of long survival. Happy the publisher when he discovers a manuscript that combines quality and popularity. Then his enthusiasm is not merely doubled, it is redoubled. Unfortunately, as we shall see, it may not be shared outside the publisher's office.

We left the manuscript in the hands of the printer. Several months will elapse before bound books are ready, and another month or six weeks between delivery of bound books and publication date. First of all, when the manuscript has been set in type, the printer supplies galley proofs. The immediate purpose of these is for the author and the proofreaders to correct errors. Authors are advised not to have afterthoughts which necessitate rewriting in the proof stage; typographical errors are corrected at the printer's expense, but most changes made by the author from the form of his original manuscript are chargeable to him, and they are expensive.

The galley proofs have another and correspondingly important purpose. They are sent out for reading by various people whose opinions, in advance of publication, will influence the reception and sale of the book. First, the publisher's own salesmen, each of whom travels in his own territory and takes orders for forthcoming books from retail and wholesale booksellers. These salesmen have been, or will be, exposed to the book at a gathering called a sales conference. With most publishers, this takes place twice a year, and the editors on the staff describe the books on the forthcoming list, which consists of a schedule of publications for six months, to the salesmen, the publicity and advertising staffs, in short to all those in the publishing organization who are concerned with getting the books to readers. Most publishers recognize only two seasons: summer and winter do not exist, so if autumn comes, spring cannot be far behind. Indeed, the sales conference for the spring list takes place in late autumn, and vice versa.

We are still within the realm where the publisher's enthusiasm is yet untested, unexposed to the chill winds of disagreement that blow outside the house. Some disagreement may exist inside the house: some members of the sales or advertising staffs may, having read a copy of the manuscript or a set of galley proofs, privately blow cold air upon the editor's opinion of a certain book. However, it is considered uncouth for negative opinions to be expressed in the sales conference itself, and the job of the salesmen and promotion staff is to try to reach the audience which the editor envisions and which he tries to describe and identify as explicitly as possible. But editors are far from infallible, and words of caution, discreetly expressed, may save the publisher from a loss incurred by manufacturing many more copies of a book than he can sell, or by spending more money for advertising than the sales revenue will support.

Other sets of galley proofs go out to recognized recipients. They are sent to book clubs for consideration as selections or alternates to be chosen for their members. They are sent to certain booksellers who may be willing to read them, and particularly to wholesale booksellers who publish advance listings of books with recommendations or other comments. Not less significantly, they are sent to *Publishers' Weekly,* a trade journal which along with news items and among other interesting features includes a selective listing and commentary on forthcoming books; and to the Virginia Kirkus Service, which covers all the books that publishers submit. This pretty well amounts to the crop, as far as books of general interest are concerned. The effect of these opinions is more predictable in general than in particular. A favorable notice in *Publishers' Weekly* is gratifying and frequently influential; but *PW* covers so few books in relation to the number published that the failure to notice a particular title may be more of a blow to the publisher's self-esteem than to the sales prospects of the book. The Virginia Kirkus Service, on the contrary, does not ignore many trade books, and its opinions are frequently unfavorable. These opinions are supposed to be sales estimates rather than literary criticisms, but a considerable amount of the latter is at least implicit and is no doubt useful to public and institutional libraries which subscribe to the service. Librarians have other channels of advance information, notably the *Library Journal,* which carries many signed reviews by qualified and experienced librarians, and the semimonthly *Booklist* of The American Library Association, which, although it is largely devoted to recommendations of books already published, reviews in each issue a few forthcoming books, likely to be in immediate demand on publication. As for the Kirkus Service reports, they may sometimes be demonstrably wrong (their negative report on *The Egg and I* was a notoriously bad prediction); and sometimes their favorable reports, like those in *PW,* give the publisher more moral than material gratification. If so, this is quite possibly the fault of the publishing industry for publishing too many books.

Very often an enthusiastic Kirkus report will give a forthcoming book just the shot it needs to make it come to life, and which the publisher's enthusiasm alone can seldom achieve—any more than the mother of a newborn baby is in a position to give it the swat on the bottom that will make it start breathing. Whatever else may be said, the advance reports of *Kirkus, Publishers' Weekly, The Booklist,* and *Library Journal* are disinterested, and accordingly indispensable.

VIII

WHAT DOES THE PUBLISHER do when his enthusiasm finds no reception but winter and rough weather? The book has been declined by all the book clubs (as most books necessarily must be); it has been ignored by everyone but Kirkus, whose reader doesn't like it. Shall the publisher pour money into advertising (he has already committed perhaps $10,000 to publish the book in the first place) in the effort to make his opinion prevail? The experience of most publishers is that this is likely to be as forlorn a hope as that of a golfer who needs a hole in one on the eighteenth to win the round. His best bet is to keep trying, *before publication,* to find outside support. At this point it is more than helpful if the author has some distinguished friends. Not that logrolling is of the essence; on the contrary, an opinion is much more valuable if it comes from an incorruptible source. The author's friends cannot be depended upon to *like* his book; but they are much easier to persuade than strangers to *read* it. There have been—conspicuously in earlier generations—men with kind hearts, too often made glad, who encouraged new writers to the point where their opinions no longer counted for much. There are always influential and distinguished people who like to read, who can be approached by publishers on behalf of a book by a writer they never heard of. Often they will share the publisher's enthusiasm, often they will not; they will always say what they think, and the publisher who sends them books must be careful not to overdo it—he must maintain their good opinion of his intelligence. These are men and women of good will, often writers themselves who remember the period of their own obscurity and who have not exchanged that obscurity for an inflated opinion of their own importance. Some writers have such an opinion, and these are too lofty to read books by unknown writers, especially in proof. But among the former, there are few if any to compare in excessive, indiscriminate lavishness of praise to the late Hugh Walpole or William Lyon Phelps, both of whom were enthusiastic about everything.

A story that does not illustrate any of the foregoing comments is nevertheless not irrelevant, and it is irresistible. To mention Hugh Walpole is to lead the discussion to Henry James, who was Walpole's friend. But a literary friendship for Henry James was a combination of personal warmth and uncompromising literary integrity. In 1910 James wrote to Walpole of the latter's new novel, *Maradick at Forty,*

. . . the whole thing is a monument to the abuse of voluminous dialogue, the absence of a plan of composition, alternation, distribution, structure, and other phases of presentation than the dialogue—so that *line* (the only thing *I* value in a fiction etc.) is replaced by a vast formless featherbediness—billows in which one sinks and is lost. And yet it's all so loveable—though not so *written.* It isn't written *at all,* darling Hugh. . . .*

* From *The Selected Letters of Henry James,* edited by Leon Edel (Farrar, Straus and Giroux).

Four years earlier he had written to Witter Bynner, declining to read a new book of stories which Bynner had sent him:

. . . if I brazenly confess that I not only haven't yet read it, but haven't even been meaning to (till your words about it thus arrive), I do no more than register the sacred truth. That sacred truth is that . . . with a long and weary experience of such matters behind me, promiscuous fiction has become abhorrent to me, and I find it the hardest thing in the world to read almost *any* new novel. Any is hard enough, but the hardest from the innocent hands of young females, young American females perhaps above all.*

The book was *The Troll Garden* by Willa Cather.

IX

TO RETURN to the publisher's problems. Here he is—here we are with an organism in gestation that started with an accepted manuscript, that has now become, in proof stage, an embryonic book. Unlike other embryos, it is visible. It can be handled. People can form opinions of it. Right now, it has been proudly displayed, but nobody likes it. So what does the publisher do? He goes ahead and publishes the book and hopes for the best— but with the background as described, there will be nothing on publication date to attract the reviewer to *this* book out of twenty-five published the same day, nothing to move the public or school librarian to order it, nothing to make the bookseller single it out for recommendation to the customers who depend upon his advice.

There is a point to be made, which was led up to by the physiological phraseology of the preceding paragraph: of all

* *Ibid.*

organisms books are the most susceptible to prenatal influence. If no one but the publisher has paid attention to a book before it is published, it will in all likelihood expire in infancy. What can be done to promote a book before publication is ten times —or twenty times—as effective as what can be done afterwards.

On publication date, the book is either born alive and kicking or stillborn, or in between. If it is an incubator baby, it still has a chance—some chance. But the book that is born with a lusty kick and shriek is the one that reviewers and booksellers will pay attention to. From here out, the book is on its own.

There are exceptions; notable among them are books designed as tools for a special purpose: how to make money, how to make weeds commit suicide, how to preserve virility after ninety, how to make everybody like you. Many of them come under the heading of what *Time,* in an access of inspired word-coinage, has called "non-books," a term that also includes a fair amount of fiction. Many others—inspirational and self-help books—are useful, at least temporarily.

Altogether in contrast to the foregoing are those books that are genuinely useful, often distinguished, that live through many publishing seasons, and indeed are the publisher's so-called backlog. These may be books that explain science to the lay public, like Amram Scheinfeld's *Your Heredity and Environment;* or that introduce the reader to the practical arts, like Sherrill Whiton's *Elements of Interior Design and Decoration* and Moreton Marsh's *The Easy Expert in Collecting and Restoring American Antiques;* or that tell people how to take care of themselves, like William A. Brams's *Managing Your Coronary* and Edward J. Stieglitz's *The Second Forty Years;* hardy perennials for the kitchen, like Louis Diat's *French Cooking for Americans,* Gladys Taber's *Stillmeadow Cook Book, The Joyce Chen Cookbook* (Chinese), and Hazel Meyer's *The Complete*

Book of Home Freezing; books for travelers, sophisticated or inexperienced, such as Harvey S. Olson's *Aboard and Abroad* (for Europe) and his *Orient Guide;* books that put us on more intimate terms with language, like *The Story of Language* and *The Story of English,* by Mario Pei, and *You English Words* by John Moore. All these books need the same kind of prenatal care and feeding as any first novel.

And this brings us to the bright side—the successful book. Some of the discussion above may have given an impression of pervading pessimism. This is far from the intention. Publishers who stay in business know their business, and their judgment of a book's possibilities is usually sound. So the typical successful book is one that has justified the publisher's enthusiasm. It has attracted enough attention before publication to make its presence felt. It gets reviewed—and if not always favorably, it provokes lively discussion. And, naturally, it is advertised.

This introduces a topic that is widely misunderstood. If advertising automatically sold books, publishers would make no mistakes. As it is, the publisher sets up an appropriation for advertising in relation to expected sales. This is a tricky business. Enthusiasm may have led to a decision at the sales conference to promise large space advertising, with layouts and schedules to be taken by the salesmen to show to their customers. Prepublication advertising may have been scheduled in the book trade journals. The publicity and library service departments may have requested, and been granted, free copies in excess of the normal appropriation (these cost money, chargeable to the advertising budget) for distribution to people who are expected to talk it up. The publisher who has spent too much of his appropriation before publication has dug a hole for himself.

On the other hand, advertising to the potential reader—to what is called the consumer, with entertaining implications of the bibliophagous—usually makes little sense unless the reader has already heard of the book. What *really* sells books, as publishers agree, is word of mouth: the recommendation by one reader to another (and how much we would all invest in a reliable Word-of-the-Mouth Club). But something has to start the tongue in the first mouth. A serial version of the book? A radio or television interview with the author? Recommendation by a librarian or bookseller who has read an advance copy or seen advance reports? Or most likely of all, a review, provocative if not favorable—and best of all, a cluster of such reviews. An advertisement? Never. (What, never? Well, hardly ever.) Advertising is the gas in the tank, not the self-starter. It will accelerate the sale of a book that is selling—it will seldom give the book its initial impetus. That is why the publisher's advertising department should resist the pressure to spend money on large space advertising until the book is published and in motion.

Publishers perpetually feel that they are being called upon to defend practices which their counterparts in other lines of business consider obsolete if not antediluvian. But publishing is different, we say, and are scoffed at for saying so by men whose financial advantages put them in a position to scoff. Well, there are certain important respects in which publishing is different, and advertising, which is the manifestation most frequently scoffed at, is one of them. A manufacturer of almost any other product—from soft drinks to automobiles—has certain advantages. His customer comes back—quickly in the case of the soft drink, less quickly but inevitably in the case of the automobile. The publisher who sells a book sells it once and for all, one to a customer. Some people buy several copies of a particular book for gifts, but the customer does not come back for the next book advertised by the publisher, which probably appeals to an altogether different taste. He may come back for the author's next book, but that will be a couple of years off. Same with automobiles? Yes, except that the automobile costs five hundred times the price of the book, and furthermore the dealer gives credit for the old car which the customer turns in. The reader, if he admires his author, wants to keep the earlier book—and he may as well, considering its trade-in value.

X

ANOTHER conspicuous feature that distinguishes book publishing from other enterprises is book reviewing. In cities from Boston and points even farther east to Los Angeles and Honolulu, newspapers review books regularly—once a week, or in New York and a few other large cities, at least a book a day, plus a weekly book section that covers dozens or scores of new titles. Many magazines, weekly and monthly, review many books. Other industries have trade journals that comment on new products, and in fact newspapers will describe new merchandise of all sorts if they think their readers are interested. Much space is given regularly to new models of automobiles. But here the space is devoted to description, not to criticism—unless there is independent criticism to be reported, as when in 1966 the subject of automobile safety was ventilated in Congress and in Mr. Ralph Nader's book, *Unsafe at Any Speed.* But Mr. Nader was not writing as a newspaper critic. Reviewers employed by newspapers and magazines, either as staff members or free lances, are expected to express their opinions of the books they review. When an opinion is unfavorable, it may cause distress to the publisher and anguish to the author, but unless it is demonstrably unfair, prejudiced, or inaccurate, publishers and experienced authors swallow their disappointment and realize that to complain in public would have the effect merely of calling attention to the original review on the part of readers who might have missed it. What other business welcomes, even invites, criticism of its products, knowing that the rough must be taken with the smooth?

What is a review for? Specifically, *whom* is it for? And what is it supposed to do for those who read it? There is a venerable definition which has acquired the characteristics of a cliché through repetition; it runs as follows. A review should answer three questions. What did the author try to do? How well did he succeed? Was it worth doing? Another axiom is that reviews are written for readers, to give them the information they require to decide what books they are interested in reading.

The trouble is that a review may admirably fulfill the foregoing functions and be dull reading itself. To be interesting, a review needs style; it should reflect a personality and still be unprejudiced. There are always some reviewers in general practice who can regularly write reviews that genuinely interest their readers and tell them how to choose what to read out of the avalanche of publications. To avoid being misinterpreted, perhaps this essay should choose its examples from reviewers who have retired from regular reviewing: Orville Prescott and John K. Hutchens; the late Joseph Henry Jackson and Lewis Gannett; Clifton Fadiman and Charles Rolo.

All these men have written regular columns or departments of newspapers or magazines. Their readers came to know their tastes and their personalities. Unlike the Phelpses and Woollcotts, whose enthusiasm was indiscriminate, they wielded all the more influence with their favorable reviews for the contrast of their frequent expressions of coolness, of distaste, sometimes of opinions altogether devastating. Quite different is the situation of the free-lance reviewer. He is called upon by the editors of magazines or of the book-review sections of newspapers to take assignments for reviewing, one book at a time; and while some free lances gain the confidence of editors sufficiently to become regular reviewers—for *The New York Times Book Review, Saturday Review, Book Week, New York Review of Books,* or whatever—even then their choice of books to review is restricted to those the editor offers them. And while there are frequent and striking exceptions, generally the influence of their reviews depends on the influence of the paper or magazine.

The converse is that the influence of the paper or magazine in book reviewing is in the long run the resultant of the abilities and standing of the individual reviewers. The book-review editor's job is not easy. When he finds a reviewer who can write professionally and interestingly, he grapples him to his stable with hoops of steel. But the editor who is trying to produce a publication that reviews books for its readers must often have occasion to feel frustration and chagrin. Even his best regular reviewers cannot always be counted upon. They go on trips; they become engrossed in their own work and have no time to spare. They get bored with an oversupply of mediocre books about which there is nothing interesting or new to say. Sooner or later, being inveterate if not compulsive readers, they discover an exciting new author, an important new book, and back they come. But meanwhile and otherwise, the editor must be looking out for new talent.

Quite obviously competitive is the review by an author of a book similar to the one under review—perhaps another treatment of the very same subject. An editor who assigns a travel book to a reviewer who has written a travel book on the same territory may delude himself that he is giving his readers an expert opinion—he is more likely to be committing an indefensible atrocity.

One obvious hunting ground is inhabited by professional writers. At least they can write. But they cannot necessarily review books by other writers. Sometimes it is difficult for a novelist to be altogether objective and impersonal about the work of a contemporary novelist. Frequently a novelist reviewing another novelist's work will overcompensate and praise lavishly. Logrolling, apparent and real, will go on as long as logs are floated to paper mills. On the other hand, a novelist reviewing another novelist's work may have too professional a point of view, and may criticize the author for not writing another kind of novel than the one he intended to write, and indeed did write. The inherent unfairness of this kind of reviewing is difficult for the reader to see through, because it is perfectly honest.

Another obvious game preserve is that of the colleges and universities. Members of college faculties are indispensable as reviewers of new books in their special fields of interest—history and biography, economics and politics, art, science, literary history and criticism. All reviewers love to review books of literary criticism and all review editors think these books are congenitally important. A vast amount of laundry exchange goes on in this area, especially among teachers of literature. Perhaps the readers outside of academic life come to feel that they *ought* to be interested. As to other subjects, most college teachers can judge a new book in their field on its merits, objectively. Not infrequently, however, professionalism has the same danger as was noted about novelists in the preceding paragraph: the author is judged by what the reviewer thinks his intentions *ought* to have been. And rare indeed is the book of history or biography written by an author who is not a college teacher—worse, not even a doctor of philosophy—that can get a fair hearing from members of the union. It would be unfair not to mention that there are notable exceptions. Allan Nevins, for instance, came to the academic world from journalism and for many years, in addition to teaching and writing his own distinguished and voluminous works, did a vast amount of reviewing, and never unfairly—indeed, he could always be interesting and fair simultaneously: a rare achievement.

Another notable instance is that of Leon Edel, who became

the leading authority on Henry James out of a career that was unacademic except for his own education at McGill University and at the Sorbonne, where, for his degree, he wrote in French a thesis published in 1931 as a full-length book, *Henry James: Les Années Dramatiques.* Most of his subsequent experience, except for his active service in World War II, was in journalism, as critic and UN correspondent, until his production in 1949 of *The Complete Plays of Henry James.* This was followed four years later by *The Untried Years,* the first volume of his four-volume biography of James. By now Mr. Edel's distinction had been widely recognized: he was invited as visiting professor to several universities and then became professor of English at New York University. The second and third volumes of his James biography, *The Conquest of London* and *The Middle Years,* were published in 1962 and in the following spring received both the National Book Award for nonfiction and the Pulitzer Prize for biography. Subsequently he has completed his edition of *The Complete Tales of Henry James,* published in twelve volumes. In 1966 New York University inaugurated the Henry James Professorship of English and American Letters with Mr. Edel as its first occupant. J.B. Lippincott Company takes pride in its association with this distinguished career, beginning with the publication of *The Complete Plays,* and looks forward to publishing the final volume of the James biography in its 175th Anniversary Year.

To return to reviewing. Many college teachers, especially those with their reputations still to make, are eager to review books. Reviewing gets their names into print; it may be the first step in publishing as an alternative to perishing. Now it goes without saying that the way to attract attention quickly is to demonstrate superiority. In book reviewing, there are only a few ways to demonstrate superiority. One is in style, another is in judgment; nothing is better than a combination of the two.

Now fastidiousness is admirable if genuine. But nothing is more easily faked. The reviewer who is too sophisticated to be taken in by what other readers admire; the reviewer who is careful not to set his own sails before he knows which way the academic wind is blowing; the reviewer who knows how to express patronizing tolerance—he is the one who can call attention to himself, to his discernment, his resistance to bluff, his fastidious superiority.

> And every one will say,
> As you walk your mystic way,
> "If that's not good enough for him which is
>   good enough for *me*,
> Why, what a very cultivated kind of youth this
>   kind of youth must be!"

Our reviewer has forgotten his Gilbert and Sullivan; so has the editor who prints his stuff.

Out of this one-upmanship there quickly develops a peck order in criticism. The critic who sees more wrong with a book than the next critic gets a higher place in the peck order. Not just *any* book—it must be a book which has been praised, is popular—and not merely popular with the undiscriminating. The thing to be superior to is the respectable and popular book-club selection, the book read with pleasure and even absorption by hundreds of thousands of readers literate but not "literary"; bookish but not critical; intelligent but not "intellectual"; cultivated* but not "cultured." These unfortunate readers have been cleverly designated as "middlebrows" in a term coined by an editor of a middlebrow magazine.

It is important to distinguish reviewing from criticism. A re-

* The connotation here being different from Gilbert's, in the quotation above, perhaps the distinction suggested between "cultivated" and "cultured" should be illustrated: a cultivated field, a cultured pearl. Anyhow, Gilbert meant "cultured" but needed the extra syllables.

view is an *ad hoc,* journalistic exercise. Its function is to relate the book to its immediate audience. Criticism goes deeper and attempts to achieve an importance beyond the immediate. Reviews are written for people who have not read the book; criticism for those who have. Reviews are ephemeral; criticism may last as long as Aristotle's *Poetics.* Therefore it is natural that academic reviewers should try to elevate their endeavors into the realm of criticism. But this is dangerous. If criticism is to have enduring value, it must be significant (in the cant word of contemporary criticism, *meaningful*) to more than an immediate audience. It should be significant to more than one generation. Criticism is at its best in the work of such distinguished men as Edmund Wilson and the late Van Wyck Brooks, in which new books seldom if ever provide the subject matter.

XI

BOOK PUBLISHING is a unique enterprise in that publishers do not control their own product. They are in partnership with their authors. It is customary for the copyright of a book to be taken out in the author's name. The author places certain rights of publication in the hands of his publisher for the duration of copyright, in return for royalties and other emoluments, as long as the book is in print. He reserves other rights—those reserved depending largely on whether the author has an agent to exploit them for him; if not, he may as well make the publisher his agent, with a division of proceeds to be fairly agreed upon. Rights open to such negotiation include serialization, foreign publication, motion picture, radio and TV adaptation. As to copyright, the technicalities are intricate; there are good books on the subject; and copyright legislation that involves sweeping changes in the present law is now pending in Congress: only one point need be mentioned here. This is the curious resistance to copyright on the part of many people who wish to quote copyright material without paying for it. This is especially true in the field of education, where the feeling seems to be that the high intention of the teachers who wish to copy for classroom use not only a few paragraphs but whole chapters of books, in order to avoid paying for the books themselves, is sufficient reason why their requests—their demands, rather—should meet with no resistance. Institutions of learning that pay for furniture and fixtures, for salaries of janitors and principals and even (though grudgingly) of teachers, assume an attitude of outraged virtue when they are told that the author and publisher of the original material did not produce it for eleemosynary purposes. Since many of the institutions whose innocence is thus injured are supported by public funds, there is a constant undercurrent of opposition to copyright on the part of some legislators (a minority, fortunately), as a matter of principle, or of its absence.

Finally, the unique condition of the book-publishing business is marked by the existence of the public library. In what other business is the customer able to go and borrow the product—for nothing, or at most for a small rental fee? (Automobiles are indeed rented, but the rental fee is substantial.) One might expect publishers to object; on the contrary, they cultivate libraries with the assiduity of college presidents cultivating rich alumni. For libraries provide a steady and dependable market, and the larger libraries must buy any book that has legitimate claims to merit.

Authors, however, do object to the unique disadvantage inherent in the very nature of their product. A theater ticket (more expensive than most books) can be used once, by one person. A book, even if bought and privately owned, can be read by the owner's family and lent to several of his friends, until it comes to rest on the shelves of one of those borrowers who never return books—and who probably never read them, either. Alternatively, it may be sold to a second-hand bookstore and go from there to a new circle of readers.

A single copy of a book in a public library may be circulated over a hundred times before it wears out; it may be consulted on the premises even more, and the author collects only one royalty. Every so often a group of authors issues a formal complaint; sometimes authors have suggested that a system be devised to compensate them for every circulation of their books by public or rental libraries. Nothing has come of these suggestions, and indeed it seems impossible to devise a practical plan from the authors' point of view. In any event, this disadvantage does not act as a deterrent to those who want to write books.

On the other hand, libraries—public, school, and college—exercise an influence on the longevity of books perhaps greater than that of any other institutions, and librarians more than any other individuals. This influence works in two ways. First and obviously, libraries keep books in their stacks long after the books have gone out of print. Secondly, and no less importantly, librarians provide a clearinghouse for opinions of new books; they, and their professional publications, somehow manage to find the center of gravity of a book and establish its enduring reputation.

This is especially true in the field of books for children. Here the need for a clearinghouse of opinion is peculiarly vital, because children's books are not ordinarily bought by children, nor are they reviewed for children. Many publications that review books (a notable exception is *The Horn Book,* in addition to magazines published principally for libraries and other institutions) lump together most if not all of their reviews of children's books in special issues published perhaps twice a year—a spring issue, and one for Children's Book Week, which comes in

November. These issues contain reviews of more books than a parent can easily digest, and the reviews themselves are likely to be too short to be very helpful. They do of course provide a medium for publishers to advertise their juveniles and are accordingly profitable for the newspapers that publish them.

Out of all this conglomeration of miscellaneous information and opinion librarians distill something intelligible. They make lists and issue bulletins. Their recommendations and advice are much sought after, not only by parents and teachers, but by editors of children's books in publishing houses. There is in fact a running collaboration between librarians and editors in the promotional activities of Children's Book Week. And at the annual convention of the American Library Association editors of children's books are conspicuously in circulation. Committees of the American Library Association issue annually a list of "Notable" children's books of the preceding year; and choose the recipients of the highly coveted Newbery and Caldecott Medals, awarded each year to the author and illustrator, respectively, of the books considered best as to text and pictures.

The fastest-growing market for books today is the school-library market. The phenomenal growth of school libraries in recent years can be attributed largely to the increase in the number of students, a natural consequence of the population explosion, and the emphasis in school courses on individual research and wide collateral reading as opposed to the use of a single textbook.

And in the light of Federally funded programs, this market will continue to expand. As an example, fiscal 1966–67 appropirations come to $105 million for books and other materials for public and parochial school libraries (under Title II of the Elementary and Secondary Education Act) and $25 million for books and other materials for college and university libraries (under Title II of the Higher Education Act).

51

XII

CHILDREN'S BOOK publishing differs significantly from publishing books for adults. The principal reason has been indicated: the child for whom the book is written is not the purchaser, the consumer is not the customer. Much of the market therefore is institutional, so much so as to influence editorial judgment and selection. A Children's Book Department will generally consist of a single editor-in-chief, with one or more assistants, and a designer. The editor-in-chief makes the decisions; the designer is responsible for the illustrations and the general appearance of the book. J. B. Lippincott Company has had the privilege of being associated with three distinguished pioneers: the late Helen Dean Fish, one of the editors who from about 1920 on shaped the character of children's book publishing; her successor, Eunice Blake, now retired; and Mary E. Harvey, also retired, who was among the first of the publishers' representatives to establish the kind of relations with librarians that now prevail.

Children's books are longer-lived than their adult counterparts. The reasons for this are varied and complex; perhaps the principal one is that many more children's books than adult books are works of imagination, a quality which does not go out of date. Indeed, most of the immortal books for whatever audience are works of imagination. This is a subject which must be left for others to explain. Whoever takes it up might also consider the question why so many of the great writers for children for the last hundred years have been English: Lewis Carroll, Beatrix Potter, Kenneth Grahame, A. A. Milne, our own Hugh Lofting and Frances Hodgson Burnett. (By a happy coincidence, the motion picture of Doctor Dolittle will be released during Lippincott's 175th Anniversary Year.)

In addition to the annual list of Notable Books for Children the American Library Association issues each spring a list of "Notable Books" for adult readers. This list usually runs to forty or fifty titles, and it might be contended that out of the twenty thousand published there are more distinguished books than the ALA list contains, and that a choice of so few must be to some extent arbitrary and capricious. Perhaps the Association believes that a longer list would be diffuse, and less useful to the small library, which can buy all the titles on the present lists each year but would not have funds to purchase twice as many, or facilities to make a choice among them. The *Booklist* of the ALA, published semimonthly, recommends even for small libraries more books than are included in the list of Notable Books. Moreover, librarians—no matter how selective their positive recommendations—are seldom censors, and their record of courage in withstanding censorious attacks on books by pressure groups all over the country has been, and continues to be, distinguished and admirable in the highest degree.

In any event, if a remedy is needed for the exclusiveness of any list, it may best be supplied by the publication of other lists by other organizations. The American Booksellers Association issues annually a list of books recommended to be kept in stock by shelf-crowded, space-hungry bookstores. Various magazines and newspapers publish their annual list. List-making is an American habit, applying to the ten best movies, the ten best-dressed women, the ten best sellers. This last can be smaller or larger, and even if it follows the decimal pattern, it is likely to be twenty—ten for fiction, ten for nonfiction. Incidentally, it may be remarked that those publications which issue best-seller lists keep their methods of arriving at the information they publish as secret as the files of the CIA.

Unlike lists of "best books," which represent opinions, best-seller lists are supposed to be factual. The relation of the lists to the facts may often be more impressionistic than scientific; they have been attacked for inaccuracy, insufficient sampling, arbitrary exclusion of certain categories of books, and the possibility that occasionally a bookseller's report may represent wish-fulfillment rather than reality.* To these criticisms the makers of best-seller lists pay perhaps as much attention as the weather does to weather prophets—and nobody does anything about either.

Best-seller lists have also been criticized for their influence in accentuating the popular book at the expense of the distinguished book; but if the appearance of a negligible book on best-seller lists increases its already substantial rate of sale, that is the responsibility of the public—in other words, it's only human. A similar criticism can be made of book clubs, but if book clubs tend to concentrate attention on too few books, the answer is that there ought to be more book clubs—and no doubt it is regrettable that certain book clubs which select books for particular tastes have not increased their general influence. Some book clubs that served useful purposes have ceased to exist. Surely the desirable object from the point of view of all concerned is to give readers digestible information and freedom of choice.

XIII

RELEVANT both to this topic and to that of literary longevity is the literary prize. The best known of the many prize awards established in this country are the Pulitzer Prizes, given an-

* Readers who wish to pursue this subject further are referred to an article by Walter Goodman, "The Truth About the Best-Seller List," in *McCall's* for November, 1966.

nually for fiction, drama, biography, history, miscellaneous non-fiction, and various categories of journalism. The Pulitzer Prizes for books and plays have inevitably been criticized—the list of awards includes many deservedly forgotten names. That would be true whoever had won the prizes. The Pulitzer Prize has made itself vulnerable in another and more serious way: the method of selection has been legitimately attacked, because the decisions of the juries have been subject to the arbitrary veto of the Trustees—or even of the President of Columbia University, who in 1941 overruled the jurors' selection of Ernest Hemingway's *For Whom the Bell Tolls* for the fiction prize on the ground, incomprehensible to anybody except the late Nicholas Murray Butler, that the novel was "licentious." Some years later a drama prize jury resigned when its choice of *Who's Afraid of Virginia Woolf?* by Edward Albee was vetoed by anonymous authorities.

Partly to counteract this effect of official pusillanimity, the National Book Awards was instituted in 1950. This institution is a creation and creature of the book industry, so called—including the American Book Publishers Council, the American Booksellers Association, and the Book Manufacturers Institute. Every March the NBA causes a meeting to be held for the announcements of its awards in the fields of fiction, poetry, and three categories of nonfiction, presided over by no less a personage than the President of Rutgers, Mason Gross. This function is well attended, by publishers and their affiliates who like parties, and who are endlessly entertained by debates among themselves to determine whether the oratory or the liquor is better.

All such functions and institutions are open to criticism, and one criticism that has been leveled at the NBA is that the spotlight cast on the prize winners, whatever good it does for them, does at least as much harm by the darkness cast upon everything else. In an attempt to meet this criticism, the National Medal for Literature was established in 1964 under the auspices of the National Book Committee, to honor the lifework of an American writer whose career has been devoted to literature. This annual award consists of a medal, accompanied by a prize of $5,000.00. Since its inception, the award has been made to Thornton Wilder and Edmund Wilson.

You can't stop prizes any more than you can stop lists, so the NBA is with us for good, along with other ornaments of our enterprise. Publishers will support them as long as they cause people to talk about books. Publishers are like Oscar Wilde at least to the point where they would prefer to have their books spoken of disparagingly rather than ignored.

In conclusion let us return to the theme of immortality: the everlasting book. Thus far we have neglected to notice the contribution to immortality made by the paperback—the so-called quality paperback, that is to say, for the popular paperback extends the audience for the original book more than it extends its life span; but even this needs qualification—surely the early Agatha Christies are enjoying a rejuvenation as well as an extension of territory. The quality paperbacks make available not only to a wide audience, but to an audience containing critics and highbrows of formidable capacities, books that were originally published—many of them by university presses—for audiences of modest dimensions. Now, particularly if the reissues of these books in paperback editions reach a college audience, captive or voluntary, the books themselves go into orbit. But in view of their physical fragility, it is impossible to conclude that immortality is the inevitable consequence of the process.

For paperbacks, like all other books, are like the gingham dog and the calico cat. Almost forty years ago, there was published *An Economic Survey of the Book Industry,* by Orion H.

Cheney, on assignment by the National Association of Book Publishers. The Association has undergone metamorphoses of character and nomenclature, but the book is still alive in a reissue. It contained a lapidary statement: BOOKS ARE CANNIBALS. This means, being interpreted, that any successful book would reach a larger audience if it were not devoured by its successors in the endless flood of overproduction.

Books, books, books, books, marching up and down again. And now, to bring the parade to an abrupt end, come the computers and the communicators, the enemies if not the successors of the book. We are told by mechanized voices that the book is an obsolescent mode of communication. This is borne in upon us by soothsayers and prophets. Their point of view is abetted by some advanced thinkers who are willing to sacrifice their community with the human race for their place in the critical and cultural peck order.

Publishers cannot afford to feel superior to their readers. It is not their place to upstage the human race. Nor do they wish to: it is necessary for the publisher to have tastes as well as taste—to recognize the best of every kind of writing. Not otherwise can he fulfill his function in the process of communication—a process in which the book will remain supreme as long as there are writers and readers with independent, unbluffable minds—who not only can bear to be alone, but who are never alone while they are in communication with each other.

—G.S.

medical
publishing

LIPPINCOTT has long been identified with medical publishing, and editors in other branches of the Company have occasionally been disconcerted by finding that physicians seem unaware that the firm publishes anything other than medical books and journals.

Medical literature is one field in which Philadelphia publishing has remained pre-eminent, and Lippincott has been one of the leading contributors in this area for almost 150 years.

The Dispensatory of the United States of America, more familiarly known as *The United States Dispensatory,* has a record of continuous publication since 1833, and the 26th Edition is to appear in 1967. This book is the oldest continuously published reference work under private ownership in the world.

During its long history the Medical Publications Division of Lippincott has published the work of practically every prominent physician and surgeon in the United States plus many from other countries.

Medical publishing is a highly specialized division of the publishing world. It tends to be concentrated under comparatively few imprints, and medical books are ordinarily marketed through highly specialized channels including subscription salesmen and medical bookstores. Most of the titles, even though of tremendous importance to the medical world, remain comparatively unknown to the general public and to trade bookstores.

One of the paradoxes of medical publishing is that very few

potential authors have the clinical experience and stature to give their writings importance and validity for practitioners. This means that competition for authors is very keen indeed. From this arises what might be called a publisher's paradox: those who have the experience are usually too busy to take time to write, and the medical publisher must devote a great deal of his time and thought to solutions to this problem.

The devices by which medical publishers have, on occasion, solved this particular problem would make interesting reading —particularly to their competitors. Most potential medical authors can be persuaded to write by one benevolent subterfuge or another.

First of all, medical educators are acutely aware of the trite but true maxim that one must publish or perish. It follows that the publisher often finds a fifth column already working within the citadel to throw open the gates to the invading publisher.

A second plan of attack which is especially effective with many practising physicians is the appeal to the humanitarianism of the practitioner. As soon as the potential author can be convinced that he has acquired valuable experience which would be of use to other physicians, he is already committed. On one occasion one of our editors turned the tide by saying with just the proper feeling in his voice: "Doctor, don't you realize that every copy of your book would save at least one life?" In contrast to writers in other fields the doctor is not primarily interested in making money from his writing. Actually, a successful specialist can make much more money by seeing additional patients than he can ever hope to make from royalties. Indeed, the great bulk of medical writing, that which is published in medical journals, is practically all done without compensation, the authors being rewarded only by a feeling of having helped their fellow physicians and possibly having advanced their own professional fortunes through referrals and similar benefits.

If return from royalties does not tempt the physician to write and if he already has a professorship, what can the wistful publisher offer? One of Lippincott's senior medical editors tells of finding the joint in the armor. Very coveted as an author (and coveted by many publishers) was a certain professor who was by far the best candidate for the authorship of a text in public health.

In conversation one day the editor remarked that he had given up hope of the professor's ever writing the desired book for any publisher, but perhaps he, the professor, out of love for his profession would look over the list of chapters for the proposed text and give the world the benefit of his wisdom by deleting, augmenting, and amending the outline. Then, when the publisher had secured as author the second, or third, or fourth best prospect, the professor might contribute a preface.

All went well. The great man consented, he read, he suggested two additional chapters and, in smoke and flames and pointed words, snorted a planted redundant chapter into nothingness. Criticism became interest, grew to involvement, and blossomed into commitment. He wrote the book. Publisher's interest begat author's interest, and it is pleasant to note that in the course of time this particular author cheerfully prepared two revisions of his book. If he ever realized how he had been snared, he never expressed resentment.

The publication of medical journals was started by J. B. Lippincott & Company in 1857 when the house launched the *Medico-Chirurgical Review* under the editorship of Samuel D. Gross. Although it achieved a wide circulation, it suspended soon after the outbreak of war in 1861. In 1870 *Medical Times* was started and found a ready acceptance. *Annals of Surgery* first appeared in 1885, the year the company was incorporated as a joint stock company under the present designation, J. B. Lippincott Company. *Annals* was acquired by the company in

1897 and continues today, full of vigor and challenge, the oldest exclusively surgical journal in the world. For the general practitioner, a quarterly journal was begun in 1891 under the title *International Clinics*. This continued until 1946. At present the Company publishes fifteen medical journals. A number of these are published for medical societies.

In the field of nursing our company assisted in the establishment of the *American Journal of Nursing*. Miss Mary E. P. Davis, chairman of a committee to find ways and means of producing the first journal for nurses in America, arranged in 1900 with Lippincott to produce the magazine and to handle all the business matters pertaining to circulation, etc. The first issue appeared in October, 1900, and the business relationship with J. B. Lippincott Company continued for twenty years.

The first nursing textbook in America, *A Hand-Book of Nursing,* was prepared under the direction of the Connecticut Training School for Nurses and was published by Lippincott in 1878. This continued through many editions. It was followed by other titles for nurses, and to this day our list has reflected our great interest and effort in the nursing field, and books for nurses have remained a very important part of Lippincott publications.

Some of the distinguished medical books which have been published by J. B. Lippincott Company are Remington: *Practice of Pharmacy;* Piersol: *Human Anatomy;* Anspach: *Gynecology;* Cushing: *The Pituitary Body and Its Disorders;* Nogushi: *Serum Diagnosis of Syphilis;* Packard: *History of Medicine in the United States;* Te Linde: *Operative Gynecology;* Bunnell: *Surgery of the Hand;* Ham: *Histology;* Allen, Harkins, Moyer and Rhoads: *Surgery: Principles and Practice;* and the many important surgical volumes of Dr. Max Thorek and Dr. Philip Thorek. In addition to the work of American authors, Lippincott has arranged for the translation and publication of many distinguished foreign works: Virchow: *Cellular Pathol-*

ogy; Keibel and Mall: *Human Embryology;* Peham and Amreich: *Operative Gynecology;* Kirschner: *Operative Surgery;* Spalteholz: *Hand Atlas of Human Anatomy;* and Fuchs: *Textbook of Ophthalmology.*

—W.K.

NEARLY EVERYBODY knows what textbooks are, but few people other than those connected with schools or the graphic arts industry have any idea about how they are conceived, published, and distributed to school systems and colleges across the country. Most parents accept textbooks as part of the school's equipment like the seats in the auditorium or the bleachers in the gymnasium. But textbooks just don't automatically appear in new schools when they are built. They are the products of a fiercely competitive textbook publishing industry. Some publishing companies publish nothing but textbooks. General publishing companies have separate divisions devoting their time and effort exclusively to the publishing of textbooks and their accompanying materials.

Since the days of Webster's *Blue Back Speller* and McGuffey's *Eclectic Readers,* textbooks, although severely criticized and often maligned, have been the mainstay of American education. The reason why no textbook will ever satisfy everybody is that textbooks attempt the impossible. Within the covers of one reasonably sized book they have to present in organized fashion an area of human knowledge that it has taken scholars thousands of volumes to explore and record. They have to reflect the latest scholarly research in their particular fields. Then they must fit their content to a particular grade level, keeping within the limitations of vocabulary and understanding appropriate to that age group. They must be "complete, accurate, and objective." They must try to avoid statements that might reasonably be considered offensive by any respectable economic, religious, racial, social, or political group in the whole United States. They cannot be too long, but at the same time they have to find room for illustrations on almost every page, be compellingly attractive in format, and at all times be interesting to the pupil. The surprising thing is that textbooks manage to do most of these things and perform their intended function in the educational process.

For sixteen years of his life a large part of every child's reading will be in textbooks. From his first ones he learns the three R's. From his last ones in college and graduate school he learns the specialized skills of his profession or the accumulated wisdom of the greatest minds our civilization has produced. From all of them he learns to interpret the culture in which he is growing up and gains some understanding of a great many things in this world that he could not possibly experience directly.

What is a textbook made of? A pound or two of paper with ink on it? Words and pictures? A glossy cloth-covered package? Within the covers, behind the words and pictures, lies the real substance of any good textbook—the idea. An author who is also an educator may have a new idea for an elementary, high school, or college textbook and go in search of a publisher. Many people are surprised, however, to learn that the textbook publisher has anything to do with the idea behind the textbook. Yet frequently the idea starts with the publisher. He decides what new educational field he is going to invade, what new and improved approach can be embodied in the book, what form of organization and format will add most to the learning process, what distinctive features must be incorporated to present the idea best. Once the idea has been formulated, the publisher must search for and select qualified educators to develop the idea, to test it in classroom situations, and to translate it into a finished manuscript. On a single textbook, two or three authors may collaborate on the writing. On a series of textbooks, teams of authors may work at various grade levels to produce the best possible manuscript for each grade. Throughout the development of the manuscripts the publisher's editor is working with the authors and is, in fact, a partner in the final product of their creative efforts.

An example of the birth of a textbook in the Educational Publishing Division of J. B. Lippincott Company is the story of *Basic Reading,* now firmly established as a successful elementary school basal reading program. Like any good textbook or series of textbooks, *Basic Reading* started with an idea—that something was wrong with the way reading was being taught from the widely used basal reading textbook series because there were far too many school children who either could not read at all or were poor readers at best. Junior high school teachers blamed the elementary school teachers for not teaching boys and girls to read. High school teachers blamed the junior high school teachers for the same thing, and college professors blamed the high school teachers. Everyone was unhappy because youngsters could not read well enough to do their schoolwork. In the late fifties the Company made the decision to enter the basal reading field but only with a new and improved approach to learning to read, a phonics-linguistics method coupled with reading selections of undisputed literary excellence. About the same time two men were joining forces to do something about trying to solve the reading problem. Glenn McCracken had been experimenting for several years with a new filmstrip approach to the teaching of reading in New Castle, Pennsylvania. McCracken's results were excellent and were beginning to attract national attention. Charles C. Walcutt of Queen's College, long a student of the English language and literature, was starting to work on a regularly organized, carefully structured phonics-linguistics method of teaching beginners to read. McCracken and Walcutt were brought together through a substantial research grant which enabled each of them to take a year's leave of absence for the purpose of visiting elementary classrooms all over the country and surveying all the existing methods being used to teach children to read. As a result of their inquiries to publishers concerning school systems to visit, Lippincott discovered the nature and extent of the McCracken and Walcutt reading research study and expressed a desire to explore the possibilities of jointly developing a new phonics-linguistics reading program with them. A year of study of the latest and most reliable reading literature, school visitations, personal conferences, and lengthy correspondence followed to hammer out the major objectives of the new program and to determine the best ways to achieve them in publishable form. With a master plan finally agreed upon, both authors and publisher began an intensive search for forward-looking reading supervisors and outstanding classroom teachers at all grade levels to prepare the teachers' manuals, word recognition cards, and workbooks to accompany the pupils' textbooks for each of the eight grades. Another two years was spent in selecting and trying out reading selections for children's interests and classroom activities to implement the learning-to-read process. Finally, the sum total of the best writing, the tested classroom experience, and the most creative thinking of everyone connected with the reading project found its way into the manuscripts of the *Basic Reading* series which were turned in to the publisher.

The example used shows how one elementary series came into being. Similar case studies could be presented to tell how new and distinctive textbooks for senior high schools and colleges in such fields as science, health, speech, social studies, and home economics were conceived and developed. More often than not, college textbooks are written by one or two authors, who are acknowledged authorities in their particular fields. Common to all textbook publishing, whether elementary, high school, or college, is the close working relationship between the author and the publisher's editor through the entire writing and preparation of the manuscript.

When the manuscript is finally received by the publisher, it is worked over by project editors who are specialists in certain subject matter areas. The content is checked for scholarship and accuracy, material is reworked and rewritten for clearer expression, artwork is prepared, photographs are selected and purchased, and style pages are designed. Finally, the publisher's editorial and production staff assemble all the various pieces and send them off to a textbook manufacturer who will take care of the composition, preparation of printing plates, printing, and binding. After composition comes a succession of sheets of galley proof, sheets of page proof, and sheets of plate proof—all of which have to be read and corrected by both the authors and the publisher's editorial staff. Months or even years after the idea was first conceived, the publisher receives his first copy of the finished textbook.

To prepare a textbook or a series of textbooks the publisher must invest thousands and thousands, sometimes hundreds of thousands, sometimes a million dollars or more of his capital before he has the copies packaged and ready for distribution. Many times, as with a series of books that must be published all at once, the publisher has his capital tied up for five years or more before he has a single copy to sell.

The first copies of any new textbook go out to the publisher's salesmen, to school people, or to college professors as samples for examination and consideration. Elaborate advertising brochures announce the publication of the new book, and packets of promotional literature are sent to salesmen and to prospective school customers. Once or twice a year the salesmen are called together for national or regional sales meetings where a new book is described in detail by the authors and the editors. The burden of all the advertising, all the promotional material for salesmen, all the speeches by authors and editors, is just about one thing—the idea that has been packaged in this textbook.

But the idea, however good, still has to be sold to the schools or colleges. The publisher's salesmen, anywhere from fifty to two hundred of them, call on the schools with the new book. They talk with college instructors, heads of departments, superintendents, supervisors, principals, and teachers. They appear before and make formal presentations to textbook selection committees composed of teachers or college faculty members. In some states they call upon members of the state board of education and their educational advisers. And throughout it all, the salesmen are persuading their listeners that the idea in the new book is superior to the ideas in their competitors' books. Because textbook salesmen sell ideas to educators, they are considered educators themselves. Most of them have been teachers. Many of them have been superintendents or principals of schools. Some have been college instructors. They often are invited to educational meetings to sit on discussion panels and to participate in workshops for the improvement of education.

Today's textbooks are not perfect. Every textbook, no matter how good, is a compromise between the ideal and the possible. No other textbooks in the world were ever made in the quantity or the quality of current American textbooks. Modern textbooks rate in beauty and in interest with their companions on the trade book shelves. Textbooks no longer are made just for the select few of high IQ and gifted potential, but instead are available for all children, teen-agers, young men and women, and adults. They are carefully planned and designed to serve today's educational needs and objectives. Textbooks will become better still when our educational system sets for itself higher goals of accomplishment and then demands even better textbooks to help reach these new goals.

—W.B.R.

1792 Establishment by Jacob Johnson of a bookstore and printing firm at 147 Market St., Philadelphia. It is believed that he ventured into publishing on a small scale.

1808 Partnership formed with Benjamin Warner. Firm known as Johnson and Warner. Later purchased outright by Warner. Publication of children's books of which many titles survive in the Rosenbach Collection, Free Library of Philadelphia.

1816 John Grigg from Kentucky joined Warner's business.

1823 John Grigg succeeded to the business upon the death of Benjamin Warner.

1830 Medical publishing division begun with publication of *Anatomy, Physiology and Diseases of the Bones and Joints,* by Dr. Samuel D. Gross.

1833 Hugh Elliot came in as a partner, and the firm name became Grigg, Elliot & Company.

1833 Publication of 1st Edition of *The Dispensatory of the United States of America,* edited by George B. Wood and Franklin Bache. With the 26th Edition published in 1967 it remains the oldest continuously published reference work under private ownership in the world.

1835 to Rapid growth of the business as book jobbers, publisher,
1849 and stationers. It became the leading medical publisher in the United States.

1850	Entire business purchased by Joshua Ballinger Lippincott, successful 36-year-old bookseller, printer, publisher of Bibles, prayer books, and general literature, located in Philadelphia at 4th and Race Streets. New partnership formed under the name of Lippincott, Grambo & Company with offices subsequently located at 20 North 4th St.
1855	Upon retirement of Henry Grambo, a former partner of Grigg, Elliot & Company, the firm was renamed J. B. Lippincott & Company.
1855	Publication of 1st Edition of *Lippincott's Pronouncing Gazetteer of the World*. Subsequent editions continued in print for almost a century thereafter.
1857	First issue of *Medico-Chirurgical Review,* edited by Dr. Samuel D. Gross. Publication suspended during the Civil War due to loss of large list of Southern States subscribers.
1858	Publication of Webster's *Blue Back Speller.*
1861	Business moved to new, larger building at 715 Market St., housing offices, complete book manufacturing plant, and retail store for books, stationery, and "fancy goods." The printing and binding facilities were the most modern in the country.
1868	First issue of *Lippincott's Magazine,* edited by Lloyd Smith, librarian of the Library Company of Philadelphia. He was succeeded by J. Foster Kirk in 1870. This magazine was published continuously by Lippincott until 1914.
1870	Publication of *Lippincott's Pronouncing Biographical Dictionary,* which continued in print in later revisions for 65 years.
1871	New York City branch office opened at 25 Bond St.

1871   Publication of *Romeo and Juliet,* first volume of the Variorum Edition of Shakespeare, edited by Dr. Horace Howard Furness.

1875   London agency established in Covent Garden to facilitate Lippincott's large book import business. This office continued in operation until 1955.

1876   Purchase of publication rights to *Worcester's Dictionary.*

1878   Publication of *A Hand-Book of Nursing,* the first nursing textbook in America.

1879   Publication of *The Writings of Albert Gallatin,* edited by Henry Adams, and *The Life of Albert Gallatin,* by Henry Adams.

1885   Business incorporated under present name of J. B. Lippincott Company, with J. B. Lippincott as president and owner.

1886   Death of J. B. Lippincott. Firm's ownership passed to his three sons, Craige, Walter, and J. Bertram. Craige Lippincott elected president, serving until his death in 1911.

1888   Publication of *The Quick or the Dead,* by Amélie Rives, the forerunner of the modern love problem novel.

1897   Lippincott became publishers of *Annals of Surgery.* First published in 1885 under editorship of Dr. Lewis Stephen Pilcher, it has continued to the present day and is now the oldest surgical journal in the world.

1897   Retail book department sold to Strawbridge & Clothier.

1897   Branch office opened in Montreal for distribution of medical publications in Canada. This business taken over in 1962 by J. B. Lippincott Company of Canada, Ltd., and moved to Toronto in 1966.

1898	Stationery and "fancy goods" department and Market St. store front sold to Lit Brothers. Lippincott business now devoted entirely to publishing—including manufacturing —books and magazines.
1899	Entire offices and manufacturing plant destroyed by fire. Only printing plates and contracts survived. Temporary quarters set up in a Philadelphia hotel.
1900	First issue of *American Journal of Nursing,* earliest journal for nurses in America. It continues to be published today in other hands.
1901	Company moved to a new five-story building erected on 6th St. facing Washington Square, housing its offices, warehouse, and manufacturing facilities. This building still contains Lippincott's main offices.
1907	Publication of *Human Anatomy,* edited by Dr. George A. Piersol.
1908	Publication of *Essentials of Medicine,* by Dr. C. P. Emerson, a standard nursing textbook for 18 editions and 55 years.
1908	Publication of *Marcia Schuyler* by Grace Livingston Hill, the first of more than 80 novels by this author over the next 40 years.
1911	Death of Craige Lippincott. Election of J. Bertram Lippincott as third president. Mr. Lippincott became chairman of the board in 1926, serving until his death in 1940.
1913	First volume of Lippincott Farm Manuals series published under editorship of Kary C. Davis.
1913	Publication of *The Woman Thou Gavest Me,* by Hall Caine, the Company's best-selling novel of the period.
1918	Establishment of a branch office in Chicago to handle school and college textbook publications.

1921   First publication of Horn-Ashbaugh Spellers.

1924   Publication of *Criminology*, by Edwin H. Sutherland, a
        college text now in its seventh edition as *Principles of
        Criminology*, with Donald R. Cressey as co-author.

1926   Election of Joseph Wharton Lippincott as fourth presi-
        dent. Mr. Lippincott became chairman of the board in
        1949 and retired in 1958.

1928   Sale of manufacturing plant. All book and magazine
        production thereafter performed by outside contractors.

1929   Publication of *Surgical Nursing*, by Dr. Eldridge L.
        Eliason.

1935   Publication of the 1st Edition of *Speech*, a high school
        speech textbook, by William Norwood Brigance and
        Wilhelmina G. Hedde.

1936   Trade editorial office opened in New York City at 250
        Park Ave. to ensure closer contact between Company's
        editorial staff and authors and agents. Office later moved
        to present quarters at 521 Fifth Ave.

1939   Publication of *Kitty Foyle*, by Christopher Morley.

1940   Purchase of Carrick and Evans, Inc., a New York pub-
        lisher of general literature. Operations merged with Lip-
        pincott's.

1941   Publication of *Crusader in Crinoline*, by Forrest Wilson,
        Pulitzer Prize-winning biography of Harriet Beecher
        Stowe.

1941   Purchase of Frederick A. Stokes Company, an old and
        distinguished New York publisher of adult and juvenile
        books, including the famous Doctor Dolittle series.
        Lippincott juvenile list thereby greatly expanded.

1941   Publication of *My Friend Flicka*, by Mary O'Hara.

1944   Publication of *Earth and High Heaven,* by Gwethalyn Graham.

1944   Establishment of Lippincott Employees' Profit Sharing Trust.

1945   Publication of *The Egg and I,* by Betty MacDonald, the largest selling trade book in the Company's history. Also *The White Tower,* by James Ramsey Ullman.

1946   Publication of *Mr. Adam,* by Pat Frank.

1949   Election of Howard K. Bauernfeind as fifth president.

1950   Publication of *Histology,* by Dr. Arthur W. Ham.

1952   Publication of *Russia: A History,* by Sidney Harcave, a college text now in its fifth edition.

1955   London agency closed. Lippincott medical and nursing publications handled in Europe and the British Commonwealth by newly formed Pitman Medical Publishing Company, Ltd.

1956   Publication of Nursing Department textbook *Fundamentals of Nursing,* by Elinor V. Fuerst and LuVerne Wolff.

1957   New Lippincott-owned corporation founded, Medical Science, Inc., to publish controlled-circulation journal *Medical Science.*

1957   Purchase of Medical Market Research, Inc., a New York corporation. Publication of *Surgery, Principles and Practice,* by Drs. Allen, Harkins, Moyer, and Rhoads.

1958   Election of Joseph W. Lippincott, Jr., as sixth president. Howard K. Bauernfeind became executive director and chairman of the board.

1960   Publication of *To Kill a Mockingbird,* by Harper Lee, 1961 Pulitzer Prize novel.

1961   Educational Division transferred from Chicago to Philadelphia. Company's complete warehousing and shipping facilities moved to rented space at 24th and Walnut Sts.

1961   Purchase of A. J. Holman Company, Bible publishers since 1801. Holman published the Revised Standard Version of the Holy Bible in 1962.

1961   Establishment of Lippincott's Preceptor series of college paperback books.

1962   Publication of *Basic Keys to Spelling* series by Theodore E. Glim and Frank S. Manchester.

1962   Purchase of E. B. Treat & Company, a New York corporation.

1962   Publication of the second and third volumes of Leon Edel's biography of Henry James, *The Conquest of London* and *The Middle Years,* 1963 Pulitzer Prize winners, and winners of the National Book Award.

1963   Publication of *Basic Reading,* a complete program of reading instruction for elementary grades, by Glenn McCracken and Charles C. Walcutt.

1965   Re-establishment of a Religious Book department in the Trade Division. First year's most successful publication was *The Comfortable Pew,* by Pierre Berton.

1966   Expansion of the College Department featuring publication of *The Western World: Renaissance to the Present,* by J. Russell Major.

1967   Company observes 175th year of publishing.